9/68

AR PTS: 0.5

SUPER BOWL SUPERSTARS

HINES WARD
and the
Pittsburgh Steelers

SUPER BOWL XL

by Michael Sandler

Consultant: Norries Wilson
Head Football Coach
Columbia University

BEARPORT
PUBLISHING

New York, New York

Credits

Cover and Title Page, © Timothy A. Clary/AFP/Getty Images; 4, © Paul Spinelli/ Getty Images; 5, © AP Images/Charlie Neibergall; 6, © Michel Setboun/Corbis; 7, © Jim Gund/Sports Illustrated; 8, © AP Images/Ric Feld; 9, © Craig Jones/ Allsport/Getty Images; 10, © AP Images/Gene J. Puskar; 11, © Heinz Kluetmeier/ Sports Illustrated; 12, © Rick Stewart/Getty Images; 13, © Al Bello/Getty Images; 14, © Al Bello/Getty Images; 15, © AP Images/Keith Srakocic; 16, © AP Images/ Michael Conroy; 17, © AP Images/David Zalubowski; 18, © Michael Fabus/ WireImage.com; 19, © AP Images/Winslow Townson; 20, © Al Tielemans/Sports Illustrated; 21, © REUTERS/You Sung-Ho; 22L, © George Gojkovich/Getty Images; 22R, © Matthew Stockman/Getty Images; 22 Background, © Andy Lyons/Getty Images.

Publisher: Kenn Goin
Senior Editor: Lisa Wiseman
Creative Director: Spencer Brinker
Design: Deborah Kaiser
Photo Researcher: Jennifer Bright

Library of Congress Cataloging-in-Publication Data

Sandler, Michael.
  Hines Ward and the Pittsburgh Steelers : Super Bowl XL / by Michael Sandler.
     p. cm. — (Super Bowl superstars)
  Includes bibliographical references and index.
  ISBN-13: 978-1-59716-538-9 (lib. bdg.)
  ISBN-10: 1-59716-538-7 (lib. bdg.)
  1. Ward, Hines, 1976—Juvenile literature. 2. Wide receivers (Football)—United States—Biography—Juvenile literature. 3. Asian American football players— Biography—Juvenile literature. 4. Super Bowl (40th : 2006 : Detroit, Mich.)— Juvenile literature. I. Title.

  GV939.W34S36 2008
  796.332092—dc22
  (B)
                                                2007006925

For more information, write to Bearport Publishing Company, Inc., 101 Fifth Avenue, Suite 6R, New York, New York 10003. Printed in the United States of America.

10 9 8 7 6 5 4 3 2 1

☆ Contents ☆

Dropping the Ball

Hines Ward jumped high into the air. He stretched out his arms to catch the pass.

The Pittsburgh Steelers' **receiver** was deep in the **end zone**. His catch would be Super Bowl XL's (40) first touchdown.

Somehow, the ball slipped right through his hands. Hines had failed to make the biggest play of his life! *It's only the second quarter,* he told himself. *I'll get another chance.*

In 2006, the Pittsburgh Steelers (left) faced the Seattle Seahawks (right) in Super Bowl XL (40).

Hines Ward has been chosen to play in the **Pro Bowl** four times.

Hines reaches for the ball, but he can't catch it.

Journey to America

Hines's journey to Super Bowl XL (40) had started thousands of miles (km) away. Hines was born in Seoul, South Korea. His mother is Korean. His father is African-American. The family moved to Georgia when Hines was one year old.

Soon after, his parents divorced. For most of his childhood, Hines was raised by his mom. Supporting a family as a single parent wasn't easy. Hines's mother often worked three jobs at a time.

Seoul, South Korea

Hines and his mother

Hines is one of very few Asian-American players in the National Football League (NFL).

Growing Up

Growing up in America wasn't easy for Hines. Classmates made fun of him for being half Korean. After a while, Hines had had enough. He decided to stop letting the other kids' teasing bother him.

Instead, he focused on his schoolwork and football. After a great high school football career, Hines became a star player at the University of Georgia.

Hines (#19) celebrates a touchdown with one of his Georgia Bulldogs teammates.

Hines playing quarterback for Georgia

At Georgia, Hines played three different positions—quarterback, running back, and most often, wide receiver.

Playing for Pittsburgh

In 1998, Hines joined the Pittsburgh Steelers. Pittsburgh was one of the NFL's greatest teams. During the 1970s, the Steelers had won four Super Bowls.

Hines worked hard to become one of the NFL's top receivers. He reminded fans of famous players such as Lynn Swann and John Stallworth.

Unlike those players, however, Hines didn't have any **Super Bowl rings**. *One year*, thought Hines, *I'll get one, too.*

San Diego Charger Vernon Fox (#36) can't hold onto Hines (#86) during a game in 2003.

Hines has caught more passes than any other receiver in Pittsburgh Steelers history.

Lynn Swann (#88) and John Stallworth (#82) each won Super Bowls with Pittsburgh.

Almost Unbeatable

Hines was sure 2004 was going to be his year. The Steelers' **passing game** was strong, led by Hines and **rookie** quarterback Ben Roethlisberger. The Steelers' **running game**, powered by Jerome Bettis, was just as good.

Pittsburgh lost just one game that season. They then rolled into the **AFC Championship Game** against the New England Patriots. Winning meant a trip to the Super Bowl. However, New England crushed Pittsburgh, 41-27.

Ben (#7), Jerome (#36), and Hines (#86) congratulate one another after a touchdown in 2004.

In 2004, Pittsburgh became the first team in AFC history to win 15 regular-season games.

Jerome's (#36) touchdown wasn't enough to win the game against the Patriots.

Pain and Promises

The loss against the Patriots was **devastating** for the players. Hines and his teammates were in tears. Jerome even talked about **retiring**.

Hines and Ben tried to change his mind. Finally, Jerome promised to return for another try at the Super Bowl.

The 2005 season, though, proved hard. Due to injuries, Pittsburgh won fewer games than the year before. As a result, they would have to play each playoff game on the road.

A disappointed Hines sits alone during the final moments of the game against the Patriots.

14

Hines (#86) scores an 85-yard (78-m) touchdown early in the 2005 season.

NFL teams with the best regular-season records are rewarded. In the playoffs, they get to play on their home fields.

Super Bowl XL (40)

Hines was usually tough under **pressure**. Yet early in the Super Bowl he seemed nervous.

He didn't have a catch the whole first quarter. His dropped pass in the second quarter cost the Steelers points. To beat the Seahawks, Hines needed to play better.

Luckily for Pittsburgh, he did. Three plays later, the ball flew toward Hines again. This time he caught it easily.

Hines before the big game

Hines's catch helped lead to a Steelers touchdown. His team led, 7-3.

MVP

Then in the fourth quarter, Hines broke the game open on an unforgettable play. It began with a handoff to running back Willie Parker. Willie then tossed the ball to wide receiver Antwaan Randle El. Antwaan fired the ball 50 yards (46 m) to Hines, who stepped into the end zone.

The dazzling touchdown locked up the 21-10 win for Pittsburgh. Afterward, Hines was named Super Bowl **MVP**.

Hines celebrates his Super Bowl win with his son, Jaden.

After the Super Bowl, Hines traveled to South Korea. On the trip, he met many **biracial** kids. He is working to help them handle the **discrimination** they often face.

Hines in South Korea

☆ Key Players ☆

There were other key players on the Pittsburgh Steelers who helped win Super Bowl XL (40). Here are two of them.

☆ Antwaan Randle El #82

Position: Wide Receiver

Born: 8/17/1979 in Riverdale, Illinois

Height: 5' 10" (1.77 m)

Weight: 192 pounds (87 kg)

Key Play: Threw the game-clinching touchdown pass to Hines; was the first receiver to throw a touchdown pass in Super Bowl history

☆ Willie Parker #39

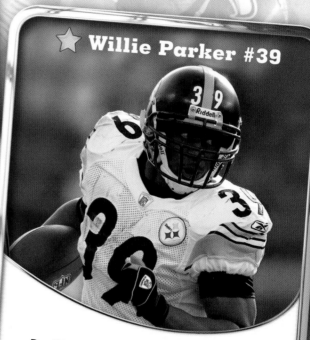

Position: Running Back

Born: 11/11/1980 in Clinton, North Carolina

Height: 5' 10" (1.77 m)

Weight: 209 pounds (95 kg)

Key Play: Made a 75-yard (69-m) touchdown run (the longest in Super Bowl history) to start the second half

☆ Glossary ☆

AFC Championship Game (AY-EFF-SEE CHAM-pee-uhn-*ship* GAME) a playoff game that decides which American Football Conference (AFC) team will go to the Super Bowl

biracial (bye-RAY-shuhl) having parents from two different races

devastating (DEV-uh-stay-ting) very hard to deal with; upsetting

discrimination (diss-*krim*-i-NAY-shuhn) the unfair treatment of people because of their race or background

end zone (END ZOHN) the area at either end of a football field where touchdowns are scored

MVP (EM-VEE-PEE) the most valuable player in a game or season

passing game (PASS-ing GAME) offensive plays that involve passing, rather than running plays

pressure (PRESH-ur) tough situations in which people might feel nervous

Pro Bowl (PROH BOHL) the NFL's all-star game that is for its very best players

receiver (ri-SEE-vur) a player whose job it is to catch passes

retiring (ri-TIRE-ing) ending one's career

rookie (RUK-ee) a player who is in his first year of NFL football

running game (RUHN-ing GAME) offensive plays that involve running, rather than passing

Super Bowl rings (SOO-pur BOHL RINGZ) rings given to players on the team that wins the Super Bowl

Bibliography

Beith, Malcolm. "Living a Dream: Hines Ward's Return to Korea." *Newsweek*, March 27, 2006.

Dillon, Dennis. "The Smiling Assassin." *The Sporting News*, February 10, 2006.

The Pittsburgh Post-Gazette

sportsillustrated.cnn.com

Read More

Buckley, James. *AFC North.* Mankato, MN: Child's World (2005).

Frisch, Aaron. *Pittsburgh Steelers: Super Bowl Champions.* Mankato, MN: Creative Education (2005).

Stewart, Mark. *The Pittsburgh Steelers.* Chicago, IL: Norwood House Press (2006).

Learn More Online

To learn more about Hines Ward, the Pittsburgh Steelers, and the Super Bowl, visit **www.bearportpublishing.com/SuperBowlSuperstars**

Index